Get set... GO!
Drawing

Ruth Thomson

Contents

CP CHILDRENS PRESS®
CHICAGO

Getting ready

It's fun to draw. Try it.
Any way you do it is a good way.

This book shows you how to use all kinds
of crayons, pens, pencils, and watercolor paints.
Then you can experiment for yourself.

Practice drawing whenever you can.
Draw things you see around you.
Draw make-believe things.
Make quick sketches.
Enjoy some quiet time drawing
slowly and carefully, as well.

Draw the same picture on smooth
paper and on rough paper.
See how different they look.

Wax crayons

Get ready

✔ Paper   ✔ Crayons

. . . Get Set

Use your crayons in different ways.
Find out how hard you need to
press down to make a heavy line.
See how fine a line you can make
by pressing lightly.
Use different-colored papers.
Do the colors look different
on different kinds of paper?

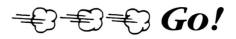 **Go!**

Use a white crayon to draw a picture
on colored paper.
Draw another picture using lots of colors.

Rubbing a doily

Get ready

✔ Paper doily ✔ Crayons ✔ Paper

. . . Get Set

Peel the paper off a crayon.
Put a sheet of paper
over a doily.
Feel where the edges
of the doily are.

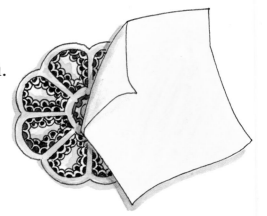

⇒🌫⇒🌫⇒🌫 *Go!*

Hold the crayon on its side
and rub it over the paper.
Hold the paper in place
with your other hand.
Watch the doily pattern appear.
Try using different colors
on top of each other.

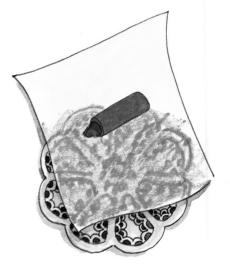

Make a crayon comb

Get ready

- ✔ Thick crayons   ✔ Paper
- ✔ Sharp knife (to be used by an adult)

. . . Get Set

Peel the paper covering
off one crayon.
Ask an adult to cut notches
along one side of the crayon.

⊰⊱⊰⊱⊰⊱ *Go!*

Hold the crayon on its side.
Move the notched edge across
a sheet of paper in circles
and twirls.
It will make patterns
of parallel lines.

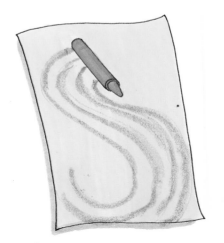

9

Chalk

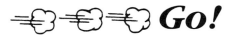

Get ready

✔ Colored chalks   ✔ A small spray bottle
✔ Paper   of fixative

. . . Get Set

Chalk is soft.
Test the colors on paper
to see how easily they blend.
Rub them with your finger.

⇒🌣⇒🌣⇒🌣 Go!

Draw a picture in chalk.
Blend some of the colors together.
Spray your picture with fixative
to keep it from smudging.

Candle drawings

Get ready

✔ White candle
✔ Colored paper
✔ Saucer

✔ Watercolor
  paint
✔ Paintbrush

. . . Get Set

Draw a picture
with the end of the candle.

≈≋ ≈≋ ≈≋ *Go!*

Brush watercolor over your
drawing. See how your picture
comes through the watercolor.
It's magical!
The picture appears because
paper absorbs watercolors,
but candle wax does not.

Crayon resists

Get ready

- ✔ Crayons
- ✔ White paper
- ✔ Watercolors
- ✔ Paintbrush

. . . Get Set

Use crayons to draw a picture.

 **Go!**

Brush a darker watercolor
lightly over the picture.
Your crayon picture
will stand out because
the wax in the crayon
does not mix with water.

15

Pens

Get ready

✔ Different kinds and colors of pens with thick, medium, and fine tips

✔ Strong, smooth paper
✔ Ruler

. . . Get Set

Test your pens.
Draw a line with each pen.
Use a ruler to guide the pen.
Which pen makes the finest line?
Try sketching with it.

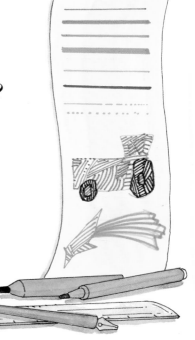

⇒☁⇒☁⇒☁ *Go!*

Draw the outline of a picture with a fine felt-tipped pen.
Color it using only lines.

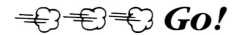

Make a paper stump

Get ready

- ✔ Long strip of paper
- ✔ Knitting needle
- ✔ Masking tape

. . . Get Set

Roll the strip of paper around and around the knitting needle. Pull the knitting needle out.

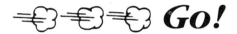 **Go!**

Tighten one end of the stump into a point.
Tape the stump
so that it cannot unroll.
Use the pointed end
for smudging and blending
chalk and crayon pictures.

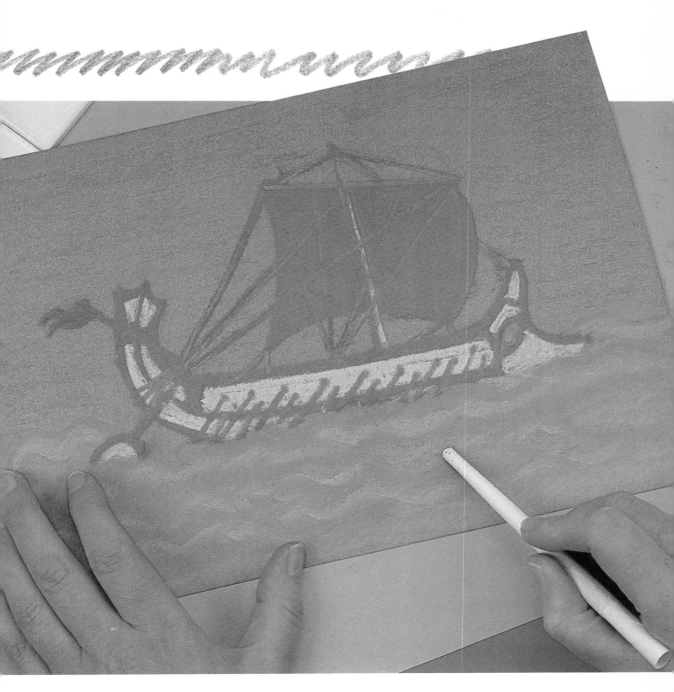

Color cutting

Get ready

- ✔ Black powder paint
- ✔ Plastic cup
- ✔ Dishwashing liquid
- ✔ Crayons
- ✔ Paintbrush
- ✔ Tablespoon
- ✔ Paper
- ✔ Teaspoon

. . . Get Set

Color the paper all over with crayons.
In a plastic cup, mix
1 tablespoon of black powder
paint with 3 tablespoons of
dishwashing liquid.
Brush the paint and dishwashing liquid mix over
the paper until the crayon is covered.

💨💨💨 *Go!*

When the paint is dry, use the teaspoon
to scrape a picture in the surface.

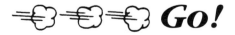

Pencils

Get ready

- ✔ Different kinds and colors of pencils
- ✔ Pencil sharpener
- ✔ Drawing paper

. . . Get Set

Make sure your pencils are sharp.
Try each one to see how thick
a line it makes.
Draw lines and patterns like this.
Lead pencils can make
different shades of grey and black
called tones.

🔊🔊🔊 *Go!*

Draw a picture with a lead pencil.
Use different tones to shade the darker areas.

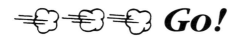

Index

Photographic credits: John Butcher, pp. 3; 23 (artwork supplied by Henry Pluckrose); Chris Fairclough Colour Library (artwork supplied by Henry Pluckrose), pp. 5, 7, 9, 11 (reproduced by permission of the Electricity Council), 13, 17, 19, 21; Henry Pluckrose, 15.

Editor: Pippa Pollard
Design: Jane Felstead
Cover design: Mike Davis
Artwork: Jane Felstead

Library of Congress Cataloging-in-Publication Data

Thomson, Ruth.
    Drawing / by Ruth Thomson.
       p.   cm. — (Get set— go!)
    Includes index.
    ISBN 0-516-07989-1
    1. Drawing—Technique—Juvenile literature. [1. Drawing—Technique.] I. Title. II. Series.
    NC655.T43   1994
    741.2—dc20   94-17329
                                                          CIP
                                                          AC

1994 Childrens Press® Edition
© 1993 Watts Books, London, New York, Sydney
All rights reserved. Printed in the United States of America.
Published simultaneously in Canada.
    2 3 4 5 6 7 8 9 0 R 03 02 01 00 99 98 97 96 95